W9-ARJ-744

Animal Friends

South Huntington Public Library
145 Pidgeon Hill Road
Huntington Station, NY 11746

BY ARNOLD RINGSTAD

Published by The Child's World®
1980 Lookout Drive • Mankato, MN 56003-1705
800-599-READ • www.childsworld.com

Acknowledgments
The Child's World®: Mary Berendes, Publishing Director
Red Line Editorial: Editorial direction
The Design Lab: Design
Amnet: Production

Photographs ©: Subbotina Anna/Shutterstock Images, cover (top),
1 (top), 18; Greg Wohlford/Erie Times-News/AP Images, cover
(center), 1 (center) 5; PhotoDisc, cover (right), 1 (right), back cover
(top left), back cover (top right), 3, 9; Shutterstock Images, back
cover (bottom), 2–3, 13, 15; Alexander Fedoroz/Rex Features/AP
Images, 4, 14; Peter Greste/TGPRN Scholastic/AP Images, 6–7;
IHA/UPPA/Photoshot/Newscom, 8; Splash News/Newscom,
11; CB2/ZOB/WENN.com/Newscom, 12; Carol Smith/Rex
Features/AP Images, 16; FoodIcons, 17; Thinkstock, 19; Adhi
Prayoga/Rex Features/AP Images, 21

Copyright © 2015 by The Child's World®
All rights reserved. No part of this book may be reproduced or
utilized in any form or by any means without written permission
from the publisher.

ISBN 9781626873575
LCCN 2014930696

Printed in the United States of America
Mankato, MN
July, 2014
PA02225

ABOUT THE AUTHOR

*Arnold Ringstad lives in
Minnesota. He has many
friends who are cats.*

CONTENTS

ANIMAL FRIENDS

Sometimes, animals form unlikely friendships. Fierce beasts and cute creatures may become friends. One such friendship happened in Pennsylvania. A gorilla at a zoo made friends with a rabbit. In Russia, a cat became friends with a chick. Read on to learn about these and other unusual animal friends.

This kitten and chick are only one example of unusual animal friends.

A Gorilla's New Pet

Gorillas are the biggest and strongest **primates**. They can weigh almost 500 pounds (225 kg). Though big and strong, gorillas are usually peaceful. They live to be very old compared to other animals. Gorillas in the zoo can live more than 50 years.

There once was an older gorilla named Samantha. She was 47 years old. Samantha lived at the Erie Zoo in Pennsylvania. Her male companion died. After seven years, her caretakers decided she needed a new friend. The friend was not a new gorilla. It was a tiny rabbit!

Surprisingly, Samantha and the rabbit became good friends. The rabbit was named Panda. It had black-and-white fur. Her caretakers said Samantha treated Panda like a favorite pet. She petted Panda on the chin. She shared food with the rabbit. Who knew a rabbit could be a gorilla's best friend?

Samantha and Panda, her unlikely friend.

Brought Together by a Tsunami

A **tsunami** is a huge wave caused by an underwater earthquake. In 2004, a powerful earthquake shook the Indian Ocean. It sent waves in all directions. Some of these waves reached Africa. One tsunami carried a group of frightened hippopotamuses out to sea.

Hippopotamuses, or hippos, spend a lot of time in the water. They are great swimmers. After the tsunami, most of the hippos swam back to land. But one baby hippo got stuck. A volunteer named Owen swam out to save him. The young hippo was named after his rescuer. Owen the hippo was scared. Volunteers brought him to an animal **sanctuary**.

The sanctuary was a new place for Owen. There were many new animals. Owen had trouble fitting in. He ran and hid behind a rock. Then, the rock started moving. It was a giant **tortoise**! The tortoise was 130 years old. Its name was Mzee. Owen and Mzee became friends. They ate and napped together until Owen grew up. Then, Owen went to live with other hippos.

Mzee helped Owen become less scared.

Adopting a Kitten

Many people have cats or dogs as pets. Some people even have both. Cats and dogs often live together. But Cotton the dog and his kitten friend have an unusual story.

Cotton adopted this gray kitten.

A cat and her young kitten lived in Bursa. Bursa is a city in the country of Turkey. One day, a mother cat was hit by a car. Her kitten became an **orphan**. A dog named Cotton found the kitten. He realized the kitten didn't have a mother. So, Cotton adopted the kitten himself.

Cotton began taking care of the kitten. Soon, the two were never apart. The pair plays and eats together. When it gets cold outside, the kitten sleeps on Cotton's back. Cotton is protective of his tiny friend. He stops anyone from getting close to the kitten!

A Speedy Cat and a Working Dog

African farmers and cheetahs don't always get along. The speedy, spotted cats are always looking for food. Cheetahs see farmers' livestock as prey. Farmers started shooting cheetahs to protect their animals. But cheetahs are **endangered**. Farmers had to come up with another way to protect their livestock.

Animal protection groups showed the farmers how to use dogs to scare the cheetahs away. The new method would not hurt the cheetahs. The groups used pairs of cheetahs and dogs to teach it to farmers. One pair was Sahara the cheetah and Alexa the dog.

Sahara and Alexa grew up together at the Cincinnati Zoo in Ohio. They liked to play and wrestle with each other. Sahara and Alexa also worked hard. Together, they helped save the lives of livestock and cheetahs.

FUN FACT
Cheetahs are the world's fastest land mammals. They can go from 0 to 60 miles per hour (96 kph) in 3 seconds. That's faster than most sports cars!

Sahara and Alexa were both friends and coworkers.

A Lion, a Tiger, and a Bear

Lions, tigers, and bears can be fierce predators in the wild. But a lion, a tiger, and a bear at an animal sanctuary in Georgia are great friends.

Leo the lion, Shere Kahn the tiger, and Baloo the black bear met as cubs. Their owner had mistreated them. They came to the sanctuary to be protected. Now, the three animals play with

Shere Kahn, Leo, and Baloo are unlikely friends.

a ball. They chase each other around. They even eat treats together.

This group would probably never occur in the wild. A worker at a nearby zoo said, "It's kind of unusual because black bears and tigers would be **solitary** as adults." In fact, the sanctuary expected them to start fighting. But they never did. The three animals live peacefully together.

Black bears usually live alone.

A Kitten and a Chick

This kitten and chick
became friends.

Cats are natural hunters. They hunt mice, bugs, birds, and other small creatures. Cats and birds are unlikely friends. But a cat and bird in Moscow, Russia, are just that.

A young girl named Maria Fedorov found a kitten out in the cold. Her parents let her keep it. The next day, Maria helped her mom go shopping. She saw a chick getting chased by a cat. She rescued the chick and brought it home. Maria's parents let her keep it, too.

Her parents worried the kitten might try to eat the tiny chick. Surprisingly, something else happened. Maria's father remembered, "Despite our fears both pets started to play with each other. They moved everywhere as twins, played, slept, and even ate together."

Chicks and kittens don't usually get along.

Going for a Deer Ride

A macaque monkey takes a ride.

The Melaka Zoo is a popular zoo in the Asian country of Malaysia. The zoo has many kinds of animals. Spotted chital deer and long-tailed macaque monkeys live there. Chital deer are from India. Macaques live all over Asia. The two animals do not live near each other in the wild. But visitors saw them being friendly at the Melaka Zoo.

Guests watched as a macaque cleaned a deer's fur. Then, the macaque climbed onto the deer's back! One guest said, "The deer was totally relaxed with this and got up and started to walk around." They stayed together for 20 minutes. People who saw them said the monkey was a very good rider. They said it was "a bit of a show off."

Finally, the monkey climbed off the deer's back. Then, it tried to find other deer to ride. No other deer would allow it.

FUN FACT
Macaques eat many different kinds of foods. Most of the time, they eat fruit. But they also eat insects and even crabs.

A Fishy Friend

Chino the dog lives with Dan and Mary Heath. The family decided to move. Their new home had a pond with fish in the back. The Heaths probably did not expect Chino to find a new friend in the pond.

Chino went to the pond every day and looked in the water. A 15-inch (38 cm) koi fish named Falstaff lived there. When Chino arrived, Falstaff would swim to the surface. Mary says, "Falstaff comes up sometimes and will nibble on Chino's paw."

His owners say that Chino always liked fish. He even looked at the ones in a tank at the **veterinarian's** office.

FUN FACT
Koi fish live a long time. Most live 25 to 30 years. Some koi live to celebrate their 200th birthday!

Now, he sits at the pond's edge. He watches Falstaff and other fish swim around. Mary says, "This is one of the few things that'll get him to wag his tail."

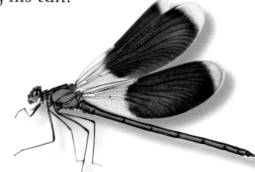

Chino finds koi fish fascinating.

The Frog and the Dragonfly

Frogs eat insects all the time. They shoot their sticky tongues out to grab flies and other bugs. One dragonfly in Indonesia did not mind getting close to a frog. It flew up to it and sat on its head.

The pair was spotted by a photographer. He saw them in his backyard. He quickly grabbed his camera and started taking pictures. He was surprised by what he saw. He said, "The frog would normally swallow the dragonfly down in one gulp, but he actually seemed quite happy for him to be sitting on his head."

The dragonfly soon flew away. The photographer was shocked by what happened next. It returned and sat on the frog! It was one lucky bug. The photographer said, "I couldn't believe how fortunate he was to have picked such a **placid** frog to land on."

This frog made a
surprising new friend.

endangered (en-DAYN-jurd) Endangered animals are at risk of dying out. Cheetahs are endangered.

orphan (OR-fun) An orphan is a child or young animal without parents. The kitten Cotton adopted was an orphan.

placid (PLA-sid) If something is placid, it is quiet and peaceful. The placid frog did not eat the dragonfly.

primates (PRY-maytz) Primates are types of mammals that include apes, monkeys, and humans. Primates such as gorillas often live in zoos.

sanctuary (SANK-chu-er-ee) A sanctuary is a place where animals are kept safe from hunters. A sanctuary protects animals.

solitary (SOL-eh-ter-ee) Being solitary means being alone. Tigers and bears are usually solitary animals.

tortoise (TOR-tis) A tortoise is a turtle that lives on land. A baby hippo became friends with a tortoise.

tsunami (soo-NAHM-ee) A tsunami is a large wave caused by an underwater earthquake. A tsunami washed hippos out to sea.

veterinarian (VET-ur-eh-NAIR-ee-un) A veterinarian is a doctor who takes care of animals. A veterinarian may have a fish tank in his or her office.

BOOKS

125 True Stories of Amazing Animals: Inspiring Tales of Animal Friendship and Four-Legged Heroes, Plus Crazy Animal Antics. Washington, DC: National Geographic, 2012.

Holland, Jennifer S. *Unlikely Friendships: 47 Remarkable Stories from the Animal Kingdom.* New York: Workman, 2011.

Shields, Amy. *Best Friends Forever! And More True Stories of Animal Friendships.* Washington, DC: National Geographic, 2013.

WEB SITES

Visit our Web site for links about animal friends:
childsworld.com/links

Note to Parents, Teachers, and Librarians:
We routinely verify our Web links to make sure they are safe and active sites. So encourage your readers to check them out!

28ᔕ0

RECEIVED FEB 2 6 2015

DISCARD